Behold, the Bridegroom Cometh

Joseph Farah

AB **ASPECT Books**
www.ASPECTBooks.com

Copyright © 2016 Joseph Farah

Copyright © 2016 Aspect Books, Inc.

ISBN-13: 978-1-4796-0705-1 (Paperback)

ISBN-13: 978-1-4796-0706-8 (ePub)

ISBN-13: 978-1-4796-0707-5 (Mobi)

Library of Congress Control Number: 2016911843

All Scripture quotations are from the King James Version (KJV).

AB **ASPECT Books**
www.ASPECTBooks.com

Table of Contents

Introduction. 5

1. The Great Disappointment 7

2. The Third Angel's Message. 9

3. The Sabbath Truth and the Sealing Message. 11

4. The Third Angel's Message and the Spirit of Prophecy 13

5. The Third Angel's Message and the Book of Joel. 16

6. The First Publishing Ventures. 20

7. The Four Generations 23

8. In the Mouth of Two or Three Witnesses. 30

9. The Fifth and Last Generation 35

10. The Secret of the Lord. 38

11. Behold, the Bridegroom Cometh 43

12. Conclusions. 51

Bibliography. 53

Introduction

As Jesus spoke upon the Mount of Olives before His crucifixion, He gave His disciples a list of definite signs that would transpire before His second coming. He afterwards declared: "When ye shall see all these things, know that it is near, even at the doors. Verily I say unto you, This generation shall not pass, till all these things be fulfilled" (Matt. 24:33, 34). Though the day and hour has not been declared to us, by a study of prophecy we may know when we have reached the generation that will not pass before Christ returns in the clouds of glory. Pioneer of the Advent movement Uriah Smith declared:

But when is this kingdom to be established? May we hope for an answer to an inquiry of such momentous concern to our race? These are the very questions on which the word of God does not leave us in ignorance; and herein is seen the surpassing value of this heavenly boon. We do not say that the exact time is revealed (we emphasize the fact that it is not) either in this or in any other prophecy; but so near an approximation is given that the generation which is to see the establishment of this kingdom may mark its approach unerringly, and make that preparation which will entitle them to share in all its glories. (Smith, *Daniel and the Revelation*, p. 65)

Is the Bible silent regarding the most climactic event of earth's history? Scripture tells us that surely the Lord will do nothing unless He first reveals it unto His servants the prophets (Amos 3:7). The prophetic word serves as a light that shines in a dark place until the day dawn and the day star arise in our hearts (2 Peter 1:19). The dawning of that day refers to the second coming of Christ in power and glory. Enough has been revealed in God's Word that we may know when we have come to the generation that will be alive at Christ's second coming.

Various authors of Scripture have foretold when "the great day of the Lord" would be near. The writings of Joel, Luke, James and Zephaniah provide prophetic signs that we may know when Jesus' coming is nigh at hand. It is important to consider that each of the ancient prophets wrote "less for their own time than for the ages to come, and especially for the generation that would live amid the last scenes of this earth's history" ("The Way, the Truth, and the Life," *The Signs of the Times*, Jan. 13, 1898). The apostle Paul wrote that everything that befell ancient Israel "happened unto them for ensamples" and "are written for our admonition upon whom the ends of the world are come" (1 Cor. 10:11).

The believer who is earnestly seeking after truth will be "constantly receiving light from heaven" ("The Stone of Witness," *The Signs of the Times*, May 26, 1881). He will not be left "in darkness that that day should overtake" him "as a thief" (1 Thess. 5:4). Ellen White wrote: "New light will ever be revealed on the word of God to him who is in living connection with the Sun of Righteousness. Let no one come to the conclusion that there is no more truth to be revealed. The diligent, prayerful seeker for truth will find precious rays of light yet to shine forth from the word of God. Many gems are yet scattered that are to be gathered together to become the property of the remnant people of God" (*Counsels to Writers and Editors*, p. 35). It is evident that the light of truth is progressive and "the path of the just is as the shining light, that shineth more and more unto the perfect day" (Prov. 4:18).

The Bible instructs and requires that we know when His coming is near, even at the door. To neglect Jesus' warning and to refuse to recognize when His advent is near will be as fatal for us as it was for those living in the days of Noah not to know when the flood was coming (*The Great Controversy*, p. 371). The purpose of this book is to demonstrate that the year 2008 was a prophetically significant year, informing us that Jesus is at the door and that this present generation shall not pass until all be fulfilled (Luke 21:32).

Chapter 1.

The Great Disappointment

In Revelation chapter 10 we read of a mighty angel coming down from heaven. He is "clothed with a cloud, and a rainbow" is "upon His head." His face resembles "the sun and His feet" are "as pillars of fire." This mighty angel who talked with John was none other than Jesus Christ (*Christ Triumphant*, p. 344). He is pictured as having in His hand an open book, which is the prophetic book of Daniel (*Manuscript Releases*, vol. 19, p. 320). When He cries with a loud voice, seven thunders utter their voices. The seven thunders were an outline of events that were to transpire under the first and second angel's message (*Manuscript Releases*, vol. 1, p. 99).

The posture of the mighty angel, with "His right foot upon the sea and His left foot on the earth," indicates that this message was to be a world-wide proclamation (Rev. 10:2). The Advent movement was not restricted to the American Northeast or to the Millerites. William Miller said, "One or two in every quarter of the globe have proclaimed the news, and all agree in the time" (Loughborough, *The Great Second Advent Movement Its Rise and Progress*, p. 105). The advent message was proclaimed in the years 1840–1844 and culminated in the Midnight Cry that commenced in the summer of 1844. When the expected time for Jesus' return passed, the Advent believers experienced a great disappointment, which was prophesied in Revelation chapter 10:

And I went unto the angel, and said unto him, Give me the little book. And he said unto me, Take it, and eat it up; and it shall make thy belly bitter, but it shall be in thy mouth sweet as honey. And I took the little book out of the angel's hand, and ate it up; and it was in my mouth sweet as honey: and as soon as I had eaten it, my belly was bitter. (Rev. 10:9, 10)

Although they were mistaken in their belief that Jesus would return in 1844, they were nonetheless led by the Spirit of God. Their calculation of the time prophecy in Daniel 8:14 was correct, but they were mistaken as to the event that was to take place. The angel informed John that the believers "must prophesy again before many peoples, and nations, and tongues, and kings" (Rev. 10:11). They had to go back and study the Bible, including the sanctuary message, and proclaim the third angel's message. Up to the time of October 22, 1844, the third angel's message was not being proclaimed. It was not until four years after the Great Disappointment that the clear light of the third angel was revealed and the proclamation of the message began.

Chapter 2.

The Third Angel's Message

As Jesus moved from the heavenly Holy Place into the heavenly Most Holy Place, He sent another angel with a third message to the world. Ellen White wrote: "As the ministration of Jesus closed in the holy place, and He passed into the holiest, and stood before the ark containing the law of God, He sent another mighty angel with a third message to the world" (*Early Writings*, p. 254).

Although the message of the third angel was sent in 1844, it was not then completely understood by the Advent believers. The period from 1844 until the third angel's message was understood was a perplexing time for them (Loughborough, p. 235). Adventist expositors of Scripture likened the truth emanating from the third angel to the rays of the sun coming over the horizon during the early dawn, when its brilliant core is not yet visible. Even in the year 1847, Joshua V. Himes declared, "The fourteenth chapter [of Revelation] presents an astounding cry [of the third angel's message], yet to be made, as a warning to mankind ..." (Loughborough, p. 247).

For the Advent believers to have fully understood the third angel's message, two important truths first had to be brought to light: the Sabbath and the "sealing message." The third angel's message is based on the idea that the Sabbath, which identifies the Creator, is the seal of God. At the time of the Great Disappointment in 1844, God in His providence directed the attention of the believers through certain verses of Scripture to the heavenly sanctuary and the Decalogue, particularly the Sabbath commandment. Revelation 14:12 reads: "Here is the patience of the saints: here are they that keep the commandments of God, and the faith of Jesus." The Advent believers needed considerable patience during their great disappointment. The latter part of the verse also directed them to the Ten Commandments as given by God.

The Great Disappointment was prophesied in Revelation 10:9–11. The verse following this passage reads: "And there was given me a reed like unto a rod: and the angel stood, saying, Rise, and measure the temple of God, and the altar, and them that worship therein" (Rev. 11:1). At the time John wrote these words, the temple in Jerusalem lay in ruins. There is no doubt that angel was directing John to "measure" the *heavenly* sanctuary. In this he encouraged believers passing through the disappointment to study carefully the events that were transpiring in the heavenly Holy Place and, starting in 1844, in the Most Holy Place.

The prophecy of Daniel 8:14 directs the attention of the reader to the cleansing of the heavenly sanctuary, which was to take place after the 2,300-day period: "And he said unto me, unto two thousand and three hundred days; then shall the sanctuary be cleansed." As believers follow Jesus into the Most Holy Place by faith, their attention is directed to the Ark of the Covenant containing the Decalogue with the Sabbath commandment at its center.

Chapter 3.

The Sabbath Truth and
the Sealing Message

One of the pioneers who first accepted the Sabbath truth was Joseph Bates (Loughborough, p. 250). His awareness of the doctrine came through a chain of witnesses. Frederick Wheeler privately embraced the Sabbath when Rachel Oakes Preston, a Seventh Day Baptist, brought it to his attention. Wheeler apparently discussed the subject with T. M. Preble, who published a pamphlet on the topic. In 1845, Bates read the pamphlet and was persuaded by its biblical evidence to keep the seventh-day Saturday, instead of the first-day Sunday, as the true Sabbath.

In 1846, Ellen White had a vision of the Most Holy Place, the Ark of the Covenant, and the tables of stone with a halo around the fourth commandment (*Early Writings*, p. 33). She saw that the Sabbath commandment was not nailed to the cross as many had taught and that God did not change the Sabbath. She saw, rather, that the Pope had substituted the first day of the week for the seventh day of the week as specified in the fourth commandment. The following year, in 1847, Ellen White received light concerning the mark of the beast:

I saw all that "would not receive the mark of the Beast, and of his Image, in their foreheads or in their hands," could not buy or sell [Rev. 13:15–17]. I saw that the number (666) of the Image Beast was made up [Rev. 13:18]; and that it was the beast that changed the Sabbath, and the Image Beast had followed on after, and kept the Pope's, and not God's Sabbath. And all we were required to do, was to give up God's Sabbath, and keep the Pope's, and then we should have the mark of the Beast, and of his image. (*A Word to the Little Flock*, p. 19)

In 1848, this little group of Adventists held a total of six Sabbath conferences. (They held six more in 1849, and ten more in 1850.) During these meetings, the Advent believers studied Scripture, and the Holy Spirit unfolded great truths to them. They formalized certain pillars of truth (Fortin, "Ellen G. White and Seventh-day Adventist Doctrines: Her role in the development of distinctive beliefs"). At the sixth conference, Ellen White had a vision regarding the "sealing truth" (Froom, *The Prophetic Faith of Our Fathers*, vol. 4, pp. 1023, 1025). She said, "At a meeting held in Dorchester, Mass., November, 1848, I had been given a view of the proclamation of the sealing message, and of the duty of the brethren to publish the light that was shining upon our pathway" (*Life Sketches of Ellen G. White*, p. 125). Elder James White, in giving his account of this meeting, wrote that Sister White described the Sabbath light as the sealing truth (*Life Sketches of Ellen G. White*, p. 116). She later wrote that the seal of the living God is contained in the third angel's message (*Manuscript Releases*, vol. 13, p. 268).

The year 1848 marked a turning point in Adventist history. By this time, the truths of the Sabbath and the "sealing message" were understood, the third angel's message was established and the way was opened for the advancement of the work (Loughborough, p. 270). Seventh-day Adventist historian W. L. Emmerson wrote that, during the Sabbath conferences, the work of uniting the believers on the great truths connected with the third angel's message commenced (Emmerson, p. 206). In 1848, the third angel's message rose to its height, and the broad, distinct disc of the message became clear as the noonday sun (Loughborough, p. 464).

Chapter 4.

The Third Angel's Message and the Spirit of Prophecy

The third angel's message is prominently featured in the writings of Ellen G. White. She declared that it is the "theme of greatest importance ... embracing the messages of the first and second angels" (*Evangelism*, p. 196). She considered it the "gospel message for these last days" (*Testimonies for the Church*, vol. 6, p. 241). She also wrote: "The present truth for this time comprises the messages, the third angel's message succeeding the first and the second" (*Manuscript Releases*, vol. 9, p. 291).

Adventist pioneer J. N. Loughborough asserted that the third angel's message was the precursor to the great Second Advent movement (Loughborough, p. vii). He called it the most solemn warning in the entire Bible, a denunciation of wrath so dreadful to which no threat can compare (Loughborough, p. 247). Ellen White wrote that it is a "fearful warning, with the most terrible threatening ever borne to man" (*Early Writings*, p. 254). Revelation 14 gives the third angel's message:

And the third angel followed them, saying with a loud voice, If any man worship the beast and his image, and receive his mark in his forehead, or in his hand, The same shall drink of the wine of the wrath of God, which is poured out without mixture into the cup of his indignation; and he shall be tormented with fire and brimstone in the presence of the holy angels, and in the presence of the Lamb: And the smoke of their torment ascendeth up for ever and ever: and they have no rest day nor night, who worship the beast and his image, and whosoever receiveth the mark of his name. Here is the patience of the saints: here are they that keep the commandments of God, and the faith of Jesus. (Rev. 14:9–12)

When John wrote, "The same shall drink of the wine of the wrath of God, which is poured out without mixture," we can understand him to mean the wrath of God unmingled with mercy. The mark of the beast is the emblem of the Papacy's authority found in the enforcement of Sunday observance. However, this is not the case at this present time. When religious and civil authorities enforce Sunday observance by law, those who choose to obey a human precept, despite the light of Scripture pointing to the true Sabbath, will receive the mark of the beast (*Evangelism*, p. 233). The question we now ask is: How will this wrath be "poured out" or manifested?

The following verses reveal that God pours out His wrath in the seven last plagues. "And I saw another sign in heaven, great and marvellous, seven angels having the seven last plagues; for in them is filled up the wrath of God" (Rev. 15:1). "And one of the four beasts gave unto the seven angels seven golden vials full of the wrath of God, who liveth for ever and ever" (Rev. 15:7). John described this great manifestation of God's wrath and the reaction of the unrighteous in Revelation 6: "And said to the mountains and rocks, Fall on us, and hide us from the face of him that sitteth on the throne, and from the wrath of the Lamb: For the great day of his wrath is come; and who shall be able to stand?" (Rev. 6:16, 17).

The phrase "great day of His wrath" is a New Testament reference to the "great day of the Lord," which the prophet Zephaniah described as "a day of wrath" (Zeph. 1:14, 15). We can deduce that the third angel's message is a warning in preparation for the day of the Lord. Consider the following exhortations through the Spirit of Prophecy: "Who are proclaiming the message of the third angel, calling the world to make ready for the great day of God?" (*Testimonies for the Church*, vol. 6, p. 166). "Sound an alarm throughout the length and breadth of the land. Tell the people that the day of the Lord is near, and hasteth greatly. Let none be left unwarned. Having heard the solemn warning of the third angel, we are debtors to others, to impart the truth to them" ("A Call to Service," *The Watchman*, June 18, 1907). "Who are voicing the message of the third angel, telling the world to make ready for the great day of God? The message we bear to the world has the seal of the living God. The Scriptures of the Old and New Testaments are to be combined in the work of fitting up a people to stand in the day of the Lord" (*Manuscript Releases*, vol. 13, p. 268).

In the next chapter, we will apply the truths of the third angel's message to the book of Joel.

Chapter 5.

The Third Angel's Message and the Book of Joel

The book of Joel in the Old Testament is a preparation for the day of the Lord. Joel, whose name means "Yahweh is God," was one of the twelve minor prophets. The book is three chapters in length, and it mentions the day of the Lord in five verses (Joel 1:15; 2:1, 11, 31; 3:14). After a brief introduction, the prophet presents this question: "Hear this, ye old men, and give ear, all ye inhabitants of the land. Hath this been in your days, or even in the days of your fathers?" (Joel 1:2).

With such an abrupt and fearful beginning, the following questions may be asked: To what message were the people to "hear" and "give ear"? To what event is the verse referring? What event was not in "their day" or "the day of their fathers"? After reading chapter one, we can draw the following conclusions:

- He talks about an unprecedented, coming calamity, an event that was unheard of to the fathers (Joel 1:2; *The Seventh-day Adventist Bible Commentary*, vol. 4, p. 939).

- He talks about devastation by a plague of locusts (Joel 1:4).

- He talks about coming judgment, which would be unparalleled in intensity and totality (Joel 1:4).

In Joel 1:2, the prophet addresses the "old men" and all the "inhabitants of the land." He addresses the same audience again in verses 14 and 15: "Sanctify ye a fast, call a solemn assembly, gather the elders and all the inhabitants of the land into the house of the Lord your God, and cry unto the Lord, Alas for the day! For the day of the Lord is at hand, and as a destruction from the Almighty shall it come." Thus, we see that Joel's message is a warning regarding the day of the Lord (Joel 1:15).

The prophet's message to Zion, to God's holy mountain, and to "all the inhabitants of the land" continues in chapter 2: "Blow ye the trumpet in Zion, and sound an alarm in my holy mountain: let all the inhabitants of the land tremble: for the day of the LORD cometh, for it is nigh at hand" (Joel 2:1).

After reading this verse, the following assessments may be made: Joel's message is an alarming warning message. The message he delivers is for all the inhabitants of the land. It is a warning that the day of the Lord approaches.

The language used by the prophet to describe the destroying locusts has striking similarities to that used by Moses in describing the plague of locusts in Egypt: "And they shall fill thy houses, and the houses of all thy servants, and the houses of all the Egyptians; which neither thy fathers, nor thy fathers' fathers have seen, since the day that they were upon the earth unto this day" (Exod. 10:6). The plague of locusts that Joel described for his day was to be of such severity that he borrowed Moses' description. Joel declares: "Hath this been in your days, or even in the days of your fathers?" (Joel 1:2). Both were events that neither they nor their fathers had ever seen. Furthermore, as Moses instructed ancient Israel to tell their son and their son's son the things that God wrought in Egypt (Exod. 10:2), so likewise did Joel command that succeeding generations be told: "Tell ye your children of it, and let your children tell their children, and their children another generation" (Joel 1:3).

Joel addressed his fearful warning to Zion and to God's holy mountain, which are references to God's people. Micah makes this connection:

But in the last days it shall come to pass, that the mountain of the house of the LORD shall be established in the top of the mountains, and it shall be exalted above the hills; and people shall flow unto it. And many nations shall come, and say, Come, and let us go up to the mountain of the LORD, and to the house of the God of Jacob; and he will teach us of his ways, and we will walk in his paths: for the law shall go forth of Zion, and the word of the LORD from Jerusalem. (Micah 4:1, 2)

Zechariah also mentioned the holy mountain as a reference to God's people. "Thus saith the LORD; I am returned unto Zion, and will dwell in the midst of Jerusalem: and Jerusalem shall be called a city of truth; and the mountain of the LORD of hosts the holy mountain" (Zech. 8:3). "Zion" and "My holy mountain" also signify the church. The apostle Paul wrote: "Now all these things happened unto them for ensamples: and they are written for our admonition, upon whom the ends of the world are come" (1 Cor. 10:11). Ellen White wrote: "The prophets spoke less for their own time than for the ages which have followed and for our own day" ("Heart Piety Essential," *The Signs of the Times*, April 2, 1896). The expression, "all the inhabitants of the land," not only refers to God's people in the entire world but to all mankind since the day of the Lord will involve all the inhabitants of the earth.

Integrating the truths that we have covered, we ask: At what point in time did Joel 1:2 speak "for our own day?" What message for our day refers to an event unheard of, which warns about the day of the Lord, makes reference to plagues, warns about the coming judgment of calamity unparalleled in intensity and totality and addresses all the inhabitants of the land? Which message are we to hear and to signal by blowing the trumpet's alarm?

The following statements from the Spirit of Prophecy provide us with insight into these questions: "We know that now everything is at stake. The third angel's message is to be at this time regarded as of the highest importance. It is a life-and-death question" (*Manuscript Releases*, vol. 9, p. 290). "The third angel's message in its clear, definite terms is to be made the prominent warning" (*Manuscript Releases*, vol. 2, p. 19). "A parchment was placed in the angel's hand, and as he descended to the earth in power and majesty, he proclaimed a fearful warning, with the most terrible threatening ever borne to man" (*Early Writings*, p. 254). "The theme of greatest importance is the third angel's message, embracing the messages of the first and second angels" (*Evangelism*, p. 196). "The third angel's message is the gospel message for these last days" (*Testimonies for the Church*, vol. 6, p. 241).

Consider the similarities between the message of Joel 2:1 and the following statement: "Sound an alarm throughout the length and breadth of the land. Tell the people that the day of the Lord is near, and hasteth greatly. Let none be left unwarned. Having heard the solemn warning of the third angel, we are debtors to others, to impart the truth to them" ("A Call to Service," *The Watchman*, June 18, 1907). Joel 2:1 reads: "Blow ye the trumpet in Zion, and sound an alarm in my holy mountain: let all the inhabitants of the land tremble: for the day of the LORD cometh, for it is nigh at hand."

The similarity of the statements would seem to indicate that Ellen White associated the third angel's message with the message of Joel. In 1848, God gave Ellen White clear light regarding the "sealing truth." She wrote: "At a meeting held in Dorchester, Mass., November, 1848, I had been given a view of the proclamation of the sealing message, and of the duty of the brethren to publish the light that was shining upon our pathway" (*Life Sketches of Ellen G. White*, p. 125). It was not until believers grasped the "sealing message" that they could properly understand the truths of the third angel's message. In 1848, the truths of the third angel's message were "very well defined, and the way was opening in different directions for the advancement of the work" (Loughborough, p. 270).

Thus, the third angel's message and Joel's message share many comparable themes. These similarities include: their reference to an event unheard of by the "fathers," their warning about the day of the Lord, their mention of a plague, their warning about coming judgment that would be unparalleled in intensity and extent, their warning about an unprecedented calamity and their addressing of all the inhabitants of the land. We are to blow a trumpet and sound an alarm for both messages as they are messages to which we are to hear and give ear.

Joel 1:2, spoken "for our own day," became present truth and was fulfilled in 1848 with the commencement of the third angel's message.

Chapter 6.

The First Publishing Ventures

Let us now turn our attention to Joel 1:3: "Tell ye your children of it, and let your children tell their children, and their children another generation." When did the first portion of the verse regarding "tell ye" become present truth? What starting date can we give it?

The word "tell" means "to give information to someone by speaking or writing" (*Merriam-Webster Dictionary*). The original Hebrew word that was used by the prophet Joel is *çâphar [saw-far']*, which means "to *score* with a mark as a tally or record, i.e. (by implication) to *inscribe*, and also to *enumerate;* intensively, to *recount*, i.e. *celebrate."* The King James translators rendered it by the words "commune, (ac-)count, declare, number, + penknife, reckon, scribe, shew forth, speak, talk, tell (out), writer" (*Strong's Concordance* #5608). A slight alteration in the root, *çephar [sefar']* means a *book*, or a roll (*Strong's Concordance* #5609). It is evident that the original word for "tell," used by the prophet, is strongly linked with writing. In fact, the word *çâphar*, in the Old Testament, is most often translated as "scribe." Used as a verb, it means "to write." As a noun, a scribe is a person who writes books or documents by hand and helps keep track of records. The profession of scribe lost most of its importance and status with the advent of printing and the dissemination of information through printed media ("Scribe," Wikipedia).

After looking at the original language used by the prophet Joel, we again present the question: When did the first portion of the verse regarding "tell ye" become present truth? What starting date can we give it? Alternatively, we may ask: At what point in the history of the church did the pioneers begin to write and publish the truths they were receiving from God? In chapter 1 of *The Publishing Ministry*, we read about the Dorchester Vision of 1848 and the "first publishing ventures." As the reader may recall, it was in Dorchester, Massachusetts, that Ellen White received a vision of the "sealing message," which clearly defined the third angel's message—the "the gospel message for these last days" (*Testimonies for the Church*, vol. 6, p. 241).

In September of 1848, James and Ellen White journeyed to Maine to attend the Topsham conference. They met with the other believers and prayed that a way might be opened to publish the truths connected with the advent message. A month later, they were assembled with a small company, including Joseph Bates, in Dorchester, Massachusetts. The small group made the publication of "the sealing message" a subject of prayer. Disputes arose among them as to what constituted the "sealing." They resolved to refer the matter to God and, after some time, in earnest prayer for light and instruction, God gave Ellen White a vision.

Ellen White described the experience: "At a meeting held in Dorchester, Mass., November, 1848, I had been given a view of the proclamation of the 'sealing message,' and of the duty of the brethren to publish the light that was shining upon our pathway." James White likewise described the gathering: "We all felt like uniting to ask wisdom from God on the points in dispute; also Brother Bates's duty in writing. We had an exceeding powerful meeting. Ellen was again taken off in vision. She then began to describe the Sabbath light, which was the sealing truth" (*Life Sketches of Ellen G. White*, p. 116, footnote).

It was because of this vision that Mrs. White encouraged her husband to leave manual labor and begin publishing, and, as he should advance by faith, success would attend his efforts. She described talking to him: "After coming out of vision, I said to my husband; I have a message for you. You must begin to print a little paper and send it out to the people" (*The Publishing Ministry*, p. 16). "The Lord would not now give him strength to labor in the field, for He had another work for him to do, and that if he ventured into the field, he would be cut down by sickness; but that he must write, write, write, and walk out by faith. He immediately began to write, and when he came to some difficult passage, we would unite in prayer to God for an understanding of the true meaning of His word." (*The Publishing Ministry*, p. 16). His first article was written and published in Middletown, Connecticut, in July of the following year and was entitled, "The Present Truth."

We have established that the spreading of the great truths connected with the third angel's message began in 1848 (Emmerson, p. 206). In that year, the truths of the third angel's message came to be "very well defined and the way was opening in different directions for the advancement of the work" (Loughborough, p. 270).

It is evident to see that Joel 1:2, 3 finds a striking parallel in the days and work of the pioneers. As we have said, Joel's writings began to speak "for our own day" at this time. The phrase "tell ye," at the beginning of Joel 1:3, refers to the "first publishing ventures" that started in 1848. The same year, the "sealing message" identified the Sabbath as the seal of God. This identification helped to define the third angel's message. Additional instruction has confirmed that we are to "tell" others of the third angel's message through the spoken and written word:

> By pen and voice we are to sound the proclamation, showing their order, and the application of the prophecies that bring us to the third angel's message. There cannot be a third without the first and second. These messages we are to give to the world in publications, in discourses, showing in the line of prophetic history the things that have been, and the things that will be. (*Manuscript Releases*, vol. 1, p. 43)

It is evident from this statement that the third angel's message is to be given through publications and discourses. Recall that the word "tell" means "to give information to someone by speaking or writing." We may further conclude that the words of Joel 1:3 "tell ye" became present truth in 1848 with the spreading of the third angel's message through the first publishing ventures, signaling when the "for our own day" began. The third angel's message is indeed the gospel message for these last days (*Testimonies for the Church*, vol. 6, p. 241).

Chapter 7.

The Four Generations

Now we will consider the latter part of Joel 1:3, which refers to four generations in the following words: "Tell ye your children of it, and let your children tell their children, and their children another generation." We can surmise that these four generations refer to God's people at the end of the world and the four generations of their prophetic history.

What is the prophetic significance of the period represented? The number four is used in various places in the Bible and carries a sense of completeness. In Genesis 15, it refers to the completion of probationary time for the Amorites: "But in the fourth generation they shall come hither again: for the iniquity of the Amorites is not yet full" (Gen. 15:16).

In 2 Kings 15, the number four is used in the sense of a testing period during which time God would determine whether King Jehu and his sons would walk in His ways: "This was the word of the LORD which he spake unto Jehu, saying, Thy sons shall sit on the throne of Israel unto the fourth generation. And so it came to pass" (2 Kings 15:12).

In Exodus 20:5, the number four is associated with God's judgment: "Thou shalt not bow down thyself to them, nor serve them: for I the LORD thy God am a jealous God, visiting the iniquity of the fathers upon the children unto the third and fourth generation of them that hate me."

In mentioning the four generations, Joel also announced to God's people that their probation was coming to an end and that the judgments of God were approaching. He further declared when God's people may know when the day of the Lord is at hand. The prophecy says, "Blow ye the trumpet in Zion, and sound an alarm in my holy mountain: let all the inhabitants of the land tremble: for the day of the LORD cometh, for it is nigh at hand." Applying it to our time, it means that there will come a definite point in time when the servants of God will know that the day of the Lord is about to break forth, and they will, in turn, give warning to the inhabitants of the earth.

The pioneers understood and believed this to be the case. J. N. Loughborough wrote: "God, by Joel, commanded, when the great day of God should be at hand" (Loughborough, p. 165). In describing the 1844 movement, Ellen White wrote: "As God by Joel commanded, when the great day of God should be at hand, it produced a rending of hearts and not of garments, and a turning unto the Lord with fasting, and weeping, and mourning" (*The Great Controversy*, p. 401). What does it mean for the day of the Lord to be at hand? To answer this question, we turn to the words of Jesus in Luke: "So likewise ye, when ye see these things come to pass, know ye that the kingdom of God is nigh at hand. Verily I say unto you, *This generation shall not pass away, till all be fulfilled*" (Luke 21:31, 32, emphasis added). Jesus used similar language as the prophet Joel in indicating when the kingdom of God should be nigh at hand. He further explained that the generation living on the earth when His kingdom should be at hand would not depart until they should see Him return in the clouds of glory. J. N. Loughborough wrote:

> In this scripture our attention is directed to the time when it is possible to learn that the coming of Christ is "at the doors" with the same assurance that we know that summer is near when we see the first tender young leaves putting forth. It may also be known that we have come to the generation which shall not pass off the stage of action until Christ himself shall come. (Loughborough, p. 93)

When Luke wrote "these things," he was referring to the signs that were to precede the second coming of Jesus. The last of the signs to be fulfilled was the "distress of nations, with perplexity" (Luke 21:25). It is evident that Ellen White believed that those who witnessed this sign, with the others, should not pass away until Christ should return. Her simplified book on the life of Christ says: "Since that time earthquakes, tempests, tidal waves, pestilence, famine, and destructions by fire and flood, have multiplied. All these, and 'distress of nations, with perplexity,' declare that the Lord's coming is near. Of those who beheld these signs He says, '... This generation shall not pass, till all these things be fulfilled'" (*The Story of Jesus*, p. 176).

At what point in history was this particular sign fulfilled? We have been instructed that the fulfillment of prophetic events has been recorded on the pages of history (*Prophets and Kings*, p. 536). The signs in the sun, moon and stars were all events that have been documented in the pages of history. The last of these signs was fulfilled in the days of the pioneers in the year 1833. Below is an outline of the events that Jesus said to look for before His coming:

Sign and Fulfillment

The times of the Gentiles: the period of the Dark Ages, from 538 to 1798

A great earthquake: the Great Lisbon Earthquake of 1755, which was felt in America

Signs in the sun: New England's Dark Day of 1780

Signs in the moon: the moon turning the color of blood in 1780

"Stars shall fall from heaven": the meteor shower of 1833

The sign of the "distress of nations, with perplexity" is mentioned only in the Gospel of Luke (21:25). Ellen White did not connect this particular sign with any past event of history. She projected the sign of the distress of nations with perplexity as an event to take place in the future:

"In the time of distress and perplexity of nations there will be many who have not given themselves wholly to the corrupting influences of the world and the service of Satan, who will humble themselves before God and turn to Him with their whole heart and find acceptance and pardon" (*Testimonies for the Church*, vol. 1, p. 268).

"In the future there will be broken thrones and great distress of nations with perplexity" (*Christ Triumphant*, p. 56).

It is for this reason that Sister White does not attach this sign to a specific event in *The Great Controversy*. Truth is progressive, and the earnest seeker will be constantly receiving light from heaven (*The Signs of the Times*, May 26, 1881). We have been instructed that "truth is an advancing truth, and we must walk in the increasing light" (*Counsels to Writers and Editors*, p. 33). Therefore, what specific situation in world events would fulfill the remaining sign—the "distress of nations, with perplexity"?

We have been told in no uncertain terms that the Bible has given us clear and distinct rays of light revealing that the day of the Lord is nigh at hand (*Counsels for the Church*, p. 64). The key to figuring out the fulfillment of this event is to search out the original meaning of the word "perplexity." The word for this in Greek is *aporia*. Liddell and Scott define it as:

I.   Of places, *difficulty of passing*

II. Of things, *difficulty, straits,* [impasse, no way out]

    2. *the not providing* a thing, *non-acquisition*

III. Of persons, *difficulty of dealing with* or *getting at*

    2. *want of means,* or *resource, a being at a loss, embarrassment, doubt, difficulty, hesitation, perplexity*

    3. ... *want of* a person or thing. (Liddell and Scott, p. 195)

The use of the word *aporia* in the verse implies that the nations of the earth are unable to meet the financial demands placed upon them. The question we now ask is: When has there been a global event on earth that there has been distress of nations with no way out of a financial predicament, with a lack of means, resources and revenue? For believers, prophecy serves as a light for the heavenward journey and that we need not to guess at anything (*The Great Controversy*, p. 598). God has instructed us that "all that prophecy has foretold as coming to pass, until the present time, has been traced on the pages of history" (*Evangelism*, p. 194). It is interesting to note, that after the 2008 global financial crisis, the former finance minister of Greece, Yanis Varoufakis, wrote a book entitled, *The Global Minotaur*. In it, he described the nations of the earth entering into a period of *aporia*. That is correct—the former finance minister of Greece uses the very ancient Greek word that the disciple Luke used. He wrote:

Nothing humanizes us like *aporia*—that state of intense puz-
zlement in which we find ourselves when our certainties fall to
pieces; when suddenly we get caught in an impasse, at a loss to
explain what our eyes can see, our fingers can touch, our ears can
hear. At those rare moments, as our reason valiantly struggles to
fathom what the senses are reporting, our *aporia* humbles us and
readies the prepared mind for previously unbearable truths. And
when the *aporia* casts its net far and wide to ensnare the whole of
humanity, we know we are at a very special moment in history.
September 2008 was just such a moment. (Varoufakis, *The Global
Minotaur*, p. 1)

Vincent Reinhart, a chief US economist at Morgan Stanley and a former secretary and economist of the Federal Open Market Committee of
the Federal Reserve, wrote a book after the Global Financial Crisis entitled, *No Way Out*. In his book, he talked about the ongoing economic crisis
and how government intervention with quantitative easing may be doing
more harm than good, inadvertently setting up the likelihood of another
financial crisis.

I believe that the last sign to precede Christ's return, the "distress of
nations, with perplexity" (Luke 21:25), was fulfilled in the great global
recession of 2008. It was in that year that "all these things" were fulfilled
and the kingdom of God was "nigh at hand" (Luke 21:31), "nigh, even at
the doors" (Mark 13:29). In describing these signs, Jesus declared: "Verily I say unto you, that this generation shall not pass, till all these things
be done" (Mark 13:30). While the other signs mentioned by the Gospel
writers represent a specific event, a more in-depth study of the "distress of
nations, with perplexity" demonstrates that it represents a "time period"
commencing in 2001 and culminating in the global financial crisis of 2008.
Ellen White alludes to the same, when she wrote: "In the time of distress and perplexity of nations there will be many ..." (*Testimonies for the
Church*, vol. 1, p. 268). As the "times of the Gentiles" represents a time
period (538–1798), so the "distress of nations, with perplexity" refers to a
time period, which I believe began in 2001, culminated in the global financial crisis of 2008 and continues to the present day. It is interesting to note
that *The Economist* of June 13, 2015, included an article entitled, "Watch
Out: It is only a matter of time before the next recession strikes." The article alludes to the fact that the financial crisis is by no means behind us. It
asserted that the surging figures of the Dow Jones are not an indication of

overall health in the economy but are merely a reflection of governmental quantitative easing. An article entitled, "IMF: The World Economy is worse off than we thought," in *CNN Money* (Jan. 20, 2015), asserts that, despite the trillions of dollars pumped into the world economy since the global financial crisis, growth is still limited.

Ellen White described an event that she associated with the "distress of nations, with perplexity." She declared: "In the future there will be broken thrones and great distress of nations with perplexity" (*Christ Triumphant*, p. 56). Among the precipitating factors that lead to revolution and the overthrow of regimes are inflation, unemployment and financial distress.

In December 2010 began the "Arab Spring," a time of uprisings that spread across the Middle East. The movement originated in Tunisia and resulted in the overthrow of the government of President Zine El Abidine Ben Ali. Next, the political unrest spread to Egypt and led to the ousting of President Hosni Mubarak. In Libya, the unrest resulted in a civil war, the overthrow of the Libyan government and the assassination of leader Muammar Gaddafi. In Yemen, the government was overthrown, and President Ali Abdullah Saleh was ousted from power. Among the remaining countries affected by the Arab Spring include Syria, Bahrain, Lebanon, Oman, Kuwait, Morocco, Sudan, Saudi Arabia, Mauritania and Jordan.

The Gospel writer Luke mentions another sign worthy of mention—"the sea and the waves roaring" (Luke 21:25). What event occurred between 2001 and 2008 that would fulfill Luke's description? No doubt the sea and waves have been roaring for centuries. However, is there an event that occurred within these eight years that matches the prediction? On December 26, 2004, the most catastrophic tidal wave ever recorded took place—the Indian Ocean tsunami, otherwise known as the Boxing Day tsunami. Its epicenter was about a 100 miles off the west coast of Sumatra, Indonesia. An earthquake of an estimated magnitude of 9.1 to 9.3 on the Richter scale precipitated the event. The earthquake affected fourteen nations and resulted in an estimated 230,000 to 280,000 deaths with many more missing.

Thus far, we have examined the writings of the disciple Luke and the Spirit of Prophecy regarding the signs preceding Christ's second advent. Having established a definition and a chronological anchor point for the term "nigh at hand," let us look at the prophetic significance of the four generations of Joel 1:3. Recall that God, by His prophet Joel, foretold when "the great day of the Lord" should be at hand. We have established that 1848 was the starting point of the spreading of the third angel's message through the first publishing ventures. If a Biblical generation is forty years, as specified in Numbers 32:13, then we may conclude that Joel's prophecy extends 160 years from 1848. Thus, we can calculate that the prophet Joel pointed to 2008 as the year when the day of the Lord became 'nigh at hand.' This view is in agreement with the prophetic sign given in the book of Luke about the "distress of nations, with perplexity" connected with Jesus' statement, "Verily I say unto you, that this generation shall not pass away, till all these things be done."

Chapter 8.

In the Mouth of Two or Three Witnesses

The apostle Paul wrote, "In the mouth of two or three witnesses shall every word be established" (2 Cor. 13:1). Are there other writers of Scripture besides the prophet Joel and the physician Luke who mention that the coming of the Lord is near? The apostle James declared: "Be ye also patient; stablish your hearts: for the coming of the Lord draweth nigh. Grudge not one against another, brethren, lest ye be condemned: behold, the judge standeth before the door" (James 5:8, 9).

A few verses earlier, James wrote: "Ye have lived in pleasure on the earth, and been wanton; ye have nourished your hearts, as in a day of slaughter" (James 5:5). The "day of slaughter" referred to here is synonymous with a "day of judgment." It is one of the many biblical references to the day of the Lord. In foretelling the destruction of spiritual Babylon, the prophet Isaiah wrote: "And there shall be upon every high mountain, and upon every high hill, rivers and streams of waters in the day of the great slaughter, when the towers fall" (Isa. 30:25). James also prophesied of the last days in the words, "Your gold and silver is cankered; and the rust of them shall be a witness against you, and shall eat your flesh as it were fire. Ye have heaped treasure together for the last days" (James 5:3). This prophecy is certainly relevant for the present time.

What type of event does James describe as indicating that the Lord's coming is near? The apostle had declared: "Go to now, ye rich men, weep and howl for your miseries that shall come upon you. Your riches are corrupted, and your garments are motheaten" (James 5:1, 2). He continued: "Behold, the hire of the labourers who have reaped down your fields, which is of you kept back by fraud, crieth: and the cries of them which have reaped are entered into the ears of the Lord of sabaoth" (James 5:4). It is evident that this divine message condemns economic greed and financial tyranny. Ellen White commented: "The Scriptures describe the condition of the world just before Christ's second coming. The apostle James pictures the greed and oppression that will prevail" ("Nearness of the End," *The Review and Herald*, March 14, 1912). Though James was addressing financial corruption in his time, his words are remarkably pertinent for our day.

We now ask: When in our day has greed prevailed? Gretchen Morgenson, a business reporter for *The New York Times*, co-authored a book about the origin of the 2008 global financial meltdown. In *Reckless Endangerment: How Outsized Ambition, Greed and Corruption Led to Economic Armageddon*, she described how regulators failed to control greed and recklessness on Wall Street. She also described how companies manipulated accounting rules, generated exorbitant salaries and bonuses for executives, used lobbying and campaign contributions to bully regulators and undertook risky financial practices that led to the crisis.

The apostle James saw that greed and oppression would reach a climax in the days preceding the coming of the Lord (*The Seventh-day Adventist Bible Commentary*, vol. 7, p. 537). "Be ye also patient; stablish your hearts: for the coming of the Lord draweth nigh. Grudge not one against another, brethren, lest ye be condemned: behold, the judge standeth before the door" (James 5:8, 9). We may conclude that James 5 meets its present-day fulfillment when greed, as condemned by the apostle, reached its climax in 2008, leading to the global financial crisis. This crisis was precipitated by greed, which Ellen White predicted would reach unprecedented proportions just before Christ's second coming.

It is worthy of mention that the apostle rebukes not only greed but also addresses extreme wealth inequality when he wrote: "Behold, the hire of the labourers who have reaped down your fields, which is of you kept back by fraud, crieth: and the cries of them which have reaped are entered into the ears of the Lord of sabaoth [the Lord of hosts]" (James 5:4). James is here describing a second phase of economic corruption.

We now ask: When, after the year 2008, has oppression prevailed in a marked way? It is interesting to note that Steven Greenhouse, a journalist with *The New York Times*, wrote an article on November 29, 2012, entitled, "With Day of Protests, Fast-Food Workers Seek More Pay." In the article, he described the biggest wave of job actions in the history of America's fast-food industry. Indeed, thousands of workers in more than a hundred cities have been protesting meager wages, and the campaigns have been growing with each successive year. NBCNews.com posted an article on December 4, 2014, entitled, "Minimum Wage Protests Hit Cities across U.S." Activists have planned demonstrations of this sort in 160 cities across the country. More recently, in the article, "Why the success of the $15 minimum wage movement has surprised its leaders," in the *Los Angeles Times* of November 11, 2015, Chris Kirkham and Samantha Masunaga reported that the job action movement has spread to 270 cities across the United States. Ellen White declared:

> By every species of oppression and extortion, men are piling up colossal fortunes, while the cries of starving humanity are coming up before God. There are multitudes struggling with poverty, compelled to labor hard for small wages, unable to secure the barest necessities of life. Toil and deprivation, with no hope of better things, make their burden heavy. When pain and sickness are added, the burden is almost unbearable. Care-worn and oppressed, they know not where to turn for relief. (*Testimonies for the Church*, vol. 9, p. 91)

Whenever, in Scripture, the cries of humanity enter into the ears of God, it is at such a time that God takes matters into His own hands. Notice God's interest in specific situations in the following passages of Scripture:

"Now therefore, behold, the cry of the children of Israel is come unto me: and I have also seen the oppression wherewith the Egyptians oppress them. Come now therefore, and I will send thee unto Pharaoh, that thou mayest bring forth my people the children of Israel out of Egypt" (Exod. 3:9, 10). "And the LORD said, Because the cry of Sodom and Gomorrah is great, and because their sin is very grievous; I will go down now, and see whether they have done altogether according to the cry of it, which is come unto me; and if not, I will know" (Gen. 18:20, 21). "And the LORD said unto Cain, Where is Abel thy brother? And he said, I know not: Am I my brother's keeper? And he said, What hast thou done? the voice of thy brother's blood crieth unto me from the ground" (Gen. 4:9, 10).

In conclusion, we have found that James described the economic state of affairs just before Christ's return. The apostle condemned the financial greed and oppression that would prevail in the last days. He spoke as much or more for our day as his own, and his prophecies have met a striking fulfillment in the global financial crisis of 2008 and the increasing waves of job actions that have been transpiring since. In view of these conditions, James declared that the coming of the Lord draws nigh and that the righteous judge is standing at the door (James 5:8, 9).

From the Gospels, it is clear that, when Jesus is at the door, the generation then living will not pass until Jesus has returned in the clouds of glory. The apostle James further declared that financial oppression would cause the cries of humanity to enter into "the ears of the Lord" of hosts (James 5:4). It is evident from Scripture that, when the cries of humanity reach the throne of God, it is time that something decisive take place and that God take matters into His own hands.

Which other writer of Holy Scripture mentions when the coming of the Lord is at hand? Turning back to the Old Testament, we read about Zephaniah's ministry in the seventh century BC, during the reign of Josiah, king of Judah. This prophet of God also warned of the nearness of day of the Lord (Zeph. 1:7). The theme of the book of Zephaniah, like that of Joel, is on "the day of the Lord." It is also not without significance that the ancestry of Zephaniah is traced back four generations (*The Seventh-day Adventist Bible Commentary*, vol. 4, p. 1062). In his writings, the prophet referred to the impending invasion of the Babylonians. However, Zephaniah's prophecies of judgment upon Judah also point to the judgments that are to fall upon an impenitent world at the time of the second advent of Christ (*Prophets and Kings*, p. 389).

In Zephaniah chapter 1, the prophet talks about the sins transpiring in Judah that led up to the day of the Lord being at hand. In verses 10 through 18, he points to the last transgression that the people were committing before divine chastisement. With the prominence of this sin, punishment was so close that the "voice" of its approach could be heard (Zeph. 1:14).

The last sins that called down the judgments of God were greed and corruption, which were prevalent in Jerusalem. We read in Zephaniah 1:10, 11: "And it shall come to pass in that day, saith the LORD, that there shall be the noise of a cry from the fish gate, and an howling from the second, and a great crashing from the hills. Howl, ye inhabitants of Maktesh, for all the merchant people are cut down; all they that bear silver are cut off."

The fish gate was one of the main centers of commerce in the city of Jerusalem. It was a place of various economic activities. The merchants not only sold fish, but many other articles of merchandise (Neh. 13:16, 20). It was a place where merchants and usurers added to their wealth through dishonest trade and unreasonably high lending rates. The prophet identified the fish gate as a place that was to be visited by God's judgments.

Zephaniah mentioned Maktesh and "all they that bear silver" in his prophecy. The word used for "bear" is *netîyl* [*net-eel'*], and it means to "lift" or "weigh." The idea carries over into the bazaar and marketplace, where exchange is made. Maktesh was a street in Jerusalem distinguished for its commerce, the counterpart of modern-day Wall Street. Its merchants would certainly have had reason to mourn when the city was made desolate. Covetousness and corruption were the order of the day as the inhabitants added to their ill-gotten gains. The prophet lamented: "Neither their silver nor their gold shall be able to deliver them in the day of the Lord's wrath" (Zeph. 1:18).

"The great day of the Lord," as prophesied by Zephaniah, met one fulfillment when Babylon destroyed Jerusalem. Yet, a greater fulfillment will take place in the final "great day of the Lord" when God destroys the entire world in judgment. The last sin pointed out by Zephaniah was financial greed and economic corruption among the inhabitants of Jerusalem.

The commercial districts of the fish gate and the street of Maktesh were singled out by the prophet to receive the retributive judgments of God. These two centers of trade serve as types of the modern-day economic greed and corruption that reached their climax in the global financial crisis of 2008. This was the year that the prophecies of Zephaniah spoke for our day, declaring when the day of the Lord will be nigh at hand.

Chapter 9.

The Fifth and Last Generation

In Joel 1:3, the prophet's message speaks to four succeeding generations. His warning "spoke for our own day," sounding forth in 1848 with the proclamation of the third angel's message through the first sabbatarian Adventist publishing ventures. It extended forward to the year 2008, at which time God's message through Joel identified when the day of the Lord should be nigh at hand (Joel 1:15; 2:1). Jesus listed specific natural and political events that were to occur, and He specified when this would be so that we might know when the kingdom of God is at hand (Luke 21:25, 31). The last sign, "distress of nations, with perplexity," likewise came to pass in 2008. Both Joel and Luke declared that the coming of the Lord would be nigh at hand in this very year. Furthermore, it was during this time that Jesus declared, "Verily I say unto you, This generation shall not pass away, till all be fulfilled" (Luke 21:32).

The next logical question is: How long is a biblical generation? According to the book of Numbers, a generation is forty years: "And the LORD's anger was kindled against Israel, and he made them wander in the wilderness forty years, until all the generation, that had done evil in the sight of the LORD, was consumed" (Num. 32:13).

As Jesus spoke on the Mount of Olives in 31 AD, He forewarned His disciples of the impending destruction of Jerusalem which took place

during that generation in the year 70 AD. It is evident that Jesus' understanding of the length of a generation is consistent with what Numbers
teaches. God kept the door of mercy open for 39 years until the very end
of that generation.

Though no man knows the day or the hour of Jesus' return, through
prophecy God has given to us a window during which we may expect the
second advent of Christ. The window period that the Lord has given to
His church in which to expect His return spans forty years, or one generation. Therefore, we may deduce that the fifth and last generation of
earth's history extends from 2008–2048. On this basis, we conclude that
we are now living in that last generation, and we will not pass off the stage
of action until Christ returns in the clouds of glory.

Does the Bible provide patterns of four generations of history for
God's people followed by the entrance into Canaan in the fifth generation? God told Abraham: "But in the fourth generation they shall come
hither again: for the iniquity of the Amorites is not yet full" (Gen. 15:16).
Levi, the son of Jacob, entered Egypt with his brethren. He begot Kohath,
who begot Amran, the father of Moses. Thus, Moses belonged to the
fourth generation, which God said would be leaving Egypt. The Bible
records that it was this generation that rebelled in the wilderness and died
before reaching the Promised Land. Their children, whom they feared
would fall prey to their enemies, were the fifth generation, which entered
into Canaan. As ancient Israel spent four generation in Egypt, so likewise
has spiritual Israel spent four generations in the world. The writings of
Ellen White identify Egypt as a symbol and representation of the world:

> Many are not growing strong, because they do not take God at his
> word. They are conforming to the world. Every day they pitch their
> tents nearer to Egypt, when they should encamp a day's march
> nearer the heavenly Canaan. ("The Christian Pathway," *Signs of
> the Times*, March 6, 1884)

As the fifth generation of ancient Israel entered Canaan, so too will
the fifth generation of spiritual Israel enter into the heavenly Canaan.
Furthermore, it is interesting to consider that, just as the ten plagues fell
upon the nation of Egypt, so likewise the seven last plagues in the book of
Revelation will be brought upon the world. Also, as God delivered ancient
Israel from the last seven of the ten plagues in Egypt, so also will He
keep spiritual Israel safe from the seven last plagues that will fall upon

the earth. God, by the prophet Isaiah, promises to conduct His remnant people safely through the great time of trouble as He led ancient Israel safely out of Egypt (*The Seventh-day Adventist Bible Commentary*, vol. 4, p. 160). Isaiah 11:15, 16 reads:

> And the LORD shall utterly destroy the tongue of the Egyptian sea; and with his mighty wind shall he shake his hand over the river, and shall smite it in the seven streams, and make men go over dryshod. And there shall be an highway for the remnant of his people, which shall be left, from Assyria; like as it was to Israel in the day that he came up out of the land of Egypt.

We conclude that each of the ancient prophets has written as much or more for our day as for their own. Their messages are applicable for the generation that lives during the closing scenes of earth's history (*The Signs of the Times*, Jan. 13, 1898). Everything that befell ancient Israel happened to them "for ensamples: and they are written for our admonition, upon whom the ends of the world are come" (1 Cor. 10:11). The word used for "ensamples" in the original Greek is *tupos* (*Strong's Concordance # 5179*). It means to serve as a *type*. The history of ancient Israel, as recorded by various authors in Scripture, serves for us as a figure, or a teaching example.

One teaching example from the history of God's people is the significance of four generations in leaving Egypt. "Four generations" serve as a type that "spoke for our own day" in 1848 with the proclamation of the third angel's message through the first sabbatarian Adventist publishing ventures. This declaration extended forward to the year 2008, at which time God, by Joel, announced when the day of the Lord should be at hand (Joel 1:15; 2:1). This is the same year in which Luke, James and Zephaniah have declared that the coming of the Lord should be nigh at hand. Jesus' declaration also applies: "Verily I say unto you, this generation shall not pass away, till all be fulfilled" (Luke 21:32). Though no man knows the day or the hour of Jesus' return, God has given us a window of time in which we *may* expect the second advent of Christ. The window of time spans forty years, or one generation. We can, therefore, conclude that the fifth and last generation of earth's history extends from 2008–2048. It is evident from this that we are living in that final generation that will not pass off the stage of action until Christ returns in the clouds of glory.

Chapter 10.

The Secret of the Lord

Jesus told His disciples that, as it was in the days of Sodom, so shall it be when the Son of man is revealed (Luke 17:30). The account of Sodom and Gomorrah serves as a type of the final destruction of the world. Did the Lord reveal to anyone His purposes regarding those cities before visiting them with judgment? The prophet Amos wrote that God will do nothing without first revealing "his secret unto his servants the prophets" (Amos 3:7). As the three heavenly visitors rose up and departed toward Sodom, Abraham started down the road with them to conduct them on their way. The Lord then said, "Shall I hide from Abraham that thing which I do?" He knew that Abraham could be trusted and that he would not betray Him. Abraham demonstrated faithfulness in keeping the way of the Lord, and God confided in him. The Lord informed him of His intentions and His purposes regarding the impending judgments of those wicked cities. It is interesting to note that the Lord later declared of Abraham: "For he is a prophet, and he shall pray for thee" (Gen. 20:7). God did, in this instance, what Amos declared—He did not do anything without first revealing "his secret unto his servants the prophets" (Amos 3:7). David taught: "The secret of the LORD is with them that fear him" (Ps. 25:14). God confided in Abraham not only because he was a prophet, but also because he was a person who feared God. The Lord declared of His servant, "For now I know that thou fearest God, seeing thou hast not withheld thy son, thine only son from me" (Gen. 22:12). Proverbs teaches: "His [God's] secret is with the righteous" (Prov. 3:32). The apostle Paul declared: "Even as Abraham believed God, and it was accounted to him for righteousness" (Gal. 3:6).

The Bible characterizes Abraham as a prophet of God who feared the Lord, and God declared him righteous as he believed in the One who had made the promise. It was for these reasons that God brought him into close connection with Himself and revealed His "secrets" regarding the cities of the plains. Thus, the destruction of Sodom and Gomorrah serves as a representation of the final destruction of the world. Abraham is a figure of God's faithful servants in the last days in whom He will confide and to whom He will declare when the day of the Lord is at hand. The secrets of the Lord have been given down through the ages to those who fear His name and have been righteous in His eyes.

To whom else has the purposes of God been revealed regarding impending judgment? Jesus stated that, as it was in the days of Noah, so shall it also be when the Son of man shall be revealed (Matt. 24:37). Hebrews says: "Being warned of God" of the coming flood, Noah, "moved with fear, prepared an ark to the saving of his house," and became an "heir of the righteousness which is by faith" (Heb. 11:7). The apostle Peter declared Noah to be "a preacher of righteousness" (2 Peter 2:5). Noah warned the inhabitants of the earth of the coming judgment of God. The Lord revealed to His servant His intention to destroy the earth because the antediluvian world was "filled with violence" (Gen. 6:13). He further said: "And behold, I, even I, do bring a flood of waters upon the earth to destroy all flesh wherein is the breath of life from under heaven; and everything that is on the earth shall die" (Gen. 6:17).

Noah is a representative of those in the last days who will be profoundly impressed by God regarding His purpose to destroy the earth by fire. Like Noah, they will heed the instructions given them and make the necessary preparations to meet the crisis while warning the inhabitants of the world.

The destruction of Jerusalem in 586 BC is a representation of the destruction that will come upon the world just before Jesus' second coming ("A Symbol of the Final Destruction," *The Signs of the Times*, Dec. 29, 1890; *Prophets and Kings*, p. 389). Among the captive Israelites during this period was Ezekiel the prophet. He was taken into exile by

King Nebuchadnezzar in 597 BC, and he prophesied in Babylon from 595 to 573 BC. His message was to draw attention to God's purpose for His people and to reveal prophecies regarding the coming destruction of Jerusalem. The Jews were not willing to cooperate with God in meeting His objectives for them as a nation, and they did not heed His warnings through Ezekiel. The Israelites mocked the servant of the Lord and responded as though the visions of judgment would not take place. They declared, "The days are prolonged, and every vision faileth" (Ezek. 12:22). God's response through Ezekiel was, "It shall be no more prolonged: for in your days, O rebellious house, will I say the word, and will perform it" (Ezek. 12:25). The generation then living would witness the judgment so long doubted and scoffed at (*The Seventh-day Adventist Bible Commentary*, vol. 4, p. 616). The prophet Ezekiel proclaimed the coming judgment of God, which came to pass in the days of those who received the warning message.

Thus, as the destruction of Jerusalem is a type or representation of the destruction of the world, so also was the prophet Ezekiel serve a representative of those God will send forth to proclaim the last warning message to the inhabitants of the earth. The generation that receives that message will witness the destruction of the world.

The prophet Habakkuk, who ministered around 600 BC, also warned of the impending invasion by the nation of Babylon. He lived during a time of deep national apostasy. Habakkuk could not understand why God permitted the crime and corruption of Judah to go unchecked. He said, "Therefore the law is slacked, and judgment doth never go forth: for the wicked doth compass about the righteous; therefore wrong judgment proceedeth" (Hab. 1:4). God informed him that He would no longer delay His divine wrath and that his generation would witness the judgment of the Lord. He declared, "Behold ye among the heathen, and regard, and wonder marvellously: for I will work a work in your days, which ye will not believe, though it be told you" (Hab. 1:5). The Lord assured him that divine wrath would come during the lifetime of those then living (*The Seventh-day Adventist Bible Commentary*, vol. 4, p. 1050). The prophecies of Habakkuk speak "for our own day," and they warn of the judgments that are to come upon the world just before the second advent of Christ (*Prophets and Kings*, p. 389). The prophet serves as a type of those in the last days who will give the final warning message to a generation who will witness the judgments of God upon an impenitent world.

The prophet Jeremiah, whose ministry started in 626 BC, was a contemporary of the prophet Habakkuk. He likewise warned of the imminent invasion of Babylon, living during a critical period of Judah's existence and witnessing the destruction of the temple and the city of Jerusalem in 586 BC. Jeremiah's ministry spanned approximately forty years, or one generation. God declared that, while Jeremiah was still in the womb, He had sanctified and ordained him "a prophet unto the nations" (Jer. 1:5). Jeremiah was raised up by God for a divine mission at a crucial time in Judah's history. His message was to reveal the sins of the people and to explain the reasons for the impending judgment. The Lord told Jeremiah, "Behold, I will cause to cease out of this place in your eyes, and in your days, the voice of mirth, and the voice of gladness, the voice of the bridegroom, and the voice of the bride" (Jer. 16:9). God warned His servant that divine judgment would be poured out in his day and that his eyes would behold it! We have made clear that the destruction of Judah by the Babylonian army is a representation of the desolation of the world during the day of the Lord (*The Great Controversy*, p. 310). The prophet Jeremiah declares:

> I beheld the earth, and, lo, it was without form, and void; and the heavens, and they had no light. I beheld the mountains, and, lo, they trembled, and all the hills moved lightly. I beheld, and, lo, there was no man, and all the birds of the heavens were fled. I beheld, and, lo, the fruitful place was a wilderness, and all the cities thereof were broken down at the presence of the LORD, and by his fierce anger. (Jer. 4:23–26)

In conclusion, as the day of the Lord approaches, God will raise up messengers to declare to the inhabitants of the world the last warning message to the generation of people who witness with their own eyes the judgments of God.

The apostle Paul described the second advent of Christ as "the blessed hope" for everyone who loves His appearing (Titus 2:13; 2 Tim. 4:8), and he added that Jesus will appear the second time without sin unto salvation to those who look for Him (Heb. 9:28). At the time of Jesus' first advent, there was a small group of humble and devout searchers of Scripture who looked for the Messiah and who believed that the appointed time of His coming had arrived. It was to these faithful believers, who were righteous before God, walking in all the commandments of the Lord blamelessly, that Heaven made known the appearance of Jesus' first coming. They had the assurance from the prophecies that their generation would see the Messiah (*The Seventh-day Adventist Bible Commentary*, vol. 5, p. 702). Simeon was among those who believed that the time appointed by God had arrived. The Scriptures describe him as just and devout and as one who waited for the consolation of Israel (Luke 2:25). The Holy Spirit revealed to him that he should not see death before he had seen the Messiah of the Lord.

The question we now ask is: Are there devout, faithful believers to whom Heaven will make known which is the generation that will see Jesus' second coming? Will there be any modern-day Simeons to whom the Holy Spirit will reveal that they should not see death before the Lord's coming? Do we have the assurance of prophecy that our generation will see the Messiah? We have been instructed that all these things happened unto them as types and that they were written for our admonition, upon whom the ends of the world are come (1 Cor. 10:11). To the believers in the last days, Jesus gave a list of prophetic signs that were to precede His second coming. He declared, "So likewise ye, when ye shall see all these things, know that it is near, even at the doors. Verily I say unto you, this generation shall not pass, till all these things be fulfilled" (Matt. 24:33, 34). These evidences from prophecy indicate when we have come to the generation that will not pass until Christ shall return in the clouds of glory. God has promised earnest seekers of truth the gift of the Holy Spirit to guide them into all truth (John 16:13). Joel taught that, before the day of the Lord, the Spirit will be poured out "upon all flesh; and your sons and your daughters shall prophesy, your old men shall dream dreams, your young men shall see visions. And also upon the servants and upon the handmaids in those days will I pour out my spirit" (Joel 2:28, 29).

A question we would do well to ask is: Should we expect a lesser manifestation of God's power just before the second advent than His Spirit demonstrated just before the first? Before the second coming, God will have a group of believers who are righteous in His eyes, walking blamelessly before Him. These will be studying the prophecies and looking for Jesus' return. It is to these faithful servants that Heaven will make known that their generation will see the appearance of Jesus in the clouds of glory.

Chapter 11.

Behold, the Bridegroom Cometh

Is the Midnight Cry only an event of the past? Is it merely a chapter in Adventist history? Or is there light from it for us today? During the Advent Movement from 1840–1844, the first angel's message went throughout the world. William Miller said, "One or two in every quarter of the globe have proclaimed the news, and all agree in the time" (Loughborough, p. 105). The Holy Spirit was moving upon the hearts and minds of many, and preachers who had never worked together were giving the message. John pronounced the first angel's message: "Saying with a loud voice, Fear God, and give glory to him; for the hour of his judgment is come: and worship him that made heaven, and earth, and the sea, and the fountains of waters" (Rev. 14:7).

This verse describes the investigative judgment—God's fair appraisal of people's choices—which commenced in 1844 and continues to the present day. History shows that the first angel's message was rejected by the majority in the churches (*Early Writings*, p. 238). As a result, they were unprepared to receive the second angel's message. During the summer of 1844, Adventists preached the second angel's message: "And there followed another angel, saying, Babylon is fallen, is fallen, that great city, because she made all nations drink of the wine of the wrath of her fornication" (Rev. 14:8).

After rejecting the first angel's message, the Protestant churches fell out of God's favor. God was calling His children out of the fallen churches that rejected the light that He had sent them. The second angel's message was empowered by the Midnight Cry, which the Adventists preached between the summer and autumn of 1844 from the words of Jesus: "And at midnight there was a cry made, Behold, the bridegroom cometh; go ye out to meet him" (Matt. 25:6).

Before the close of human probation, the first, second and third angel's messages will be proclaimed again along with the "loud cry" of Revelation 18. We now ask: Will there be another "midnight cry"? If the message is to sound forth once again, how does it relate to the three angels' messages and the "loud cry" of Revelation 18? Furthermore, what was the message of the Midnight Cry? God has instructed us that the parable of the ten virgins "has been and will be fulfilled to the very letter, for it has a special application to this time" ("The Righteousness of Christ," *The Review and Herald*, Aug. 19, 1890). The Midnight Cry, which was given between the summer and autumn of 1844, was proclaimed, in the very words of Scripture, "Behold, the Bridegroom cometh!" (*The Great Controversy*, p. 398). The proclamation was not given in the words or wisdom of humanity, but according to the word of God and through the power of His Holy Spirit. There is inherent power in God's word. By faith, we believe that the heavens and earth came into existence by the word of God (2 Peter 3:5). God has told us that one verse of Scripture is of more value than ten thousand of man's ideas or arguments (*Counsels on Health*, p. 254). When God's servants proclaim this message, they will not be giving their ideas or opinions about the Midnight Cry. They will be preaching God's Word in their own individuality.

The Midnight Cry was a message proclaimed in the very words of Scripture. So we ask: To whom was it addressed? In the parable, the message was given to the ten virgins who are a representation of the church (*Christ's Object Lessons*, p. 407). The fact that the Bible refers to them as virgins indicates that they profess the pure faith. These professed followers of Jesus are not mixed up with the erroneous teachings of Babylon. They do not heed the traditions and maxims of man that are in direct contradiction to the Word of God. It is important to recognize that the lamp in the possession of each virgin represents the Bible (*Christ's Object Lessons*, p. 407). David declares in Psalms 119:105, "Thy word is a lamp unto my feet, and a light unto my path." It is evident, therefore, that this group believes in *sola scriptura* and are advocates of the truth.

The fact that there are ten virgins is also significant. The number ten in the Bible signifies completeness and perfection. We have, for example, God's Ten Commandments, to which nothing can be added or taken away. The ten virgins profess to have faith, not only in the pure truth but also in the complete truth, which includes the Decalogue and the Sabbath commandment at its center. As the virgins were waiting for the return of the bridegroom, they represent Christians who profess to be looking for the return of Jesus Christ.

Now, based on the characteristics of the ten virgins, we ask: What particular denomination might they represent? Which church professes to believe the pure and complete truth, including all Ten Commandments in the Decalogue? Which church advocates what the Bible teaches about the second advent of Jesus? It is evident that this parable has a distinctive application for God's last-day remnant people, for Seventh-day Adventist who keep all of God's commandments in faith.

The Midnight Cry message will be God's wake-up call for Seventh-day Adventists to warn them of events regarding the close of earth's history and the nearness of Jesus' coming.

We now ask: Who gave the message? If all ten virgins were asleep, who gave the "midnight cry"? Ellen White mentioned that it was a "company who walked in the light" who will proclaim the message:

> Had all who claimed to believe the truth acted their part as wise virgins, the message would ere this have been proclaimed to every nation, kindred, tongue, and people. But five were wise and five were foolish. The truth should have been proclaimed by the ten virgins, but only five had made the provision essential to join that company who walked in the light that had come to them. (*Manuscript Releases*, vol. 16, p. 268)

Upon hearing the message, those who had sufficient oil were able to join themselves to this group. In his letter to the Thessalonians, Paul used similar language in writing to the believers concerning the times and seasons of the Lord's return. The apostle makes reference to the "children of light," who neither slumber nor sleep. 1 Thessalonians 5:4, 5 reads: "Ye are all the children of light, and the children of the day: we are not of the night, nor of darkness. Therefore let us not sleep, as do others; but let us watch and be sober." It is this select group who watch for the approaching day of the Lord and will warn others of the nearness of Jesus' coming.

The Midnight Cry will be proclaimed by a body of Christians who are described as a "company who walked in the light." God will send His servants to wake up the sleeping church members and declare to them the nearness of the coming of the Bridegroom.

The question we must now ask is: Where will the Bridegroom be coming? In one application, the message refers to the second advent of Jesus (*Christ's Object Lessons*, p. 421). The pioneers proclaimed the Midnight Cry, announcing the imminent coming of their Lord. In a second application, it refers to the Bridegroom coming to the marriage (Matt. 25:10; *The Great Controversy*, p. 427). So, where does the marriage take place? Ellen White mentioned that it would be celebrated in the Most Holy Place in heaven after Jesus ceases His work of intercession (*Early Writings*, p. 251). Ellen White also mentioned that the marriage will be to the New Jerusalem (*Early Writings*, p. 251). Revelation 21:9, 10 reads:

> And there came unto me one of the seven angels which had the seven vials full of the seven last plagues, and talked with me, saying, Come hither, I will show thee the bride, the Lamb's wife. And he carried me away in the spirit to a great and high mountain, and showed me that great city, the holy Jerusalem, descending out of heaven from God.

The virgins that go out to meet the bridegroom are a symbol of the church, who are the guests at the marriage supper (*The Great Controversy*, p. 427). So then, if the marriage takes place in heaven, how are they said to go into the marriage? It is evident that they cannot be present in person but must enter the marriage by faith (*The Great Controversy*, p. 427).

The Midnight Cry announces the arrival of the Bridegroom to the marriage in heaven before He returns to earth. When is this message to be given? It is evident that, according to the parable, the cry went forth at midnight (Matt. 25:6). The midnight hour represents the darkest hour of this earth's history (*Christ's Object Lessons*, p. 414). This particular time is brought about by the many deceptions, errors, heresies and delusions of the last days (*Christ's Object Lessons*, p. 414). We have also been instructed that the "great apostasy" will develop into darkness deep as midnight (*Christ's Object Lessons*, p. 414). The prophet Isaiah described a similar state of affairs that would take place in the world at the first advent: "For, behold, the darkness shall cover the earth, and gross darkness the people: but the LORD shall arise upon thee, and his glory shall be seen upon thee" (Isa. 60:2).

It was man's doctrines, dogmas, maxims, traditions, errors and long, intricate explanations that precipitated the gross darkness ("Christ, the Teacher of Righteousness," The *Review and Herald*, Aug. 6, 1895). It is evident that the factors producing the spiritual darkness at Jesus' first coming will also be responsible for the darkness present when He returns.

So, what event, error, deception, tradition of man, dogma, delusion or doctrine of man will plunge this country into the "great apostasy," or "national apostasy," and will lead to darkness as deep as midnight? Ellen White warned that the implementation of a national Sunday law will result in "national apostasy," which will bring "national ruin" (*Last Day Events*, p. 133). The exaltation of the Sunday Sabbath in place of the Bible Sabbath has been described as the last act in the drama (*Last Day Events*, p. 136). Thus, it is the passing of a national Sunday law that will plunge this country into the "great apostasy", or "national apostasy," which will lead to darkness as deep as midnight. It will be at this time that the Midnight Cry will be proclaimed by the company of light to arouse the sleeping church members to the important issues that will decide their eternal destiny. Thus, the Midnight Cry is a message designed by God to wake up the church during the darkest hour of earth's history.

Are there other important issues addressed by the Midnight Cry? The message is also a reminder of the need for self-examination. Sister White wrote: "The message was heart-searching, leading the believers to seek a living experience for themselves. They knew that they could not lean upon one another" (*Early Writings*, p. 238). When all the "virgins arose and trimmed their lamps," "the foolish said unto the wise": "Give us of your oil; for our lamps are gone out" (Matt. 25:8). The response of the wise to the foolish was that they could not share their oil and have enough for their own needs. They told the foolish virgins to go to the oil sellers and buy for themselves. The meaning of the parable is that the experience of the wise virgins could not suffice for them and the foolish virgins too. The symbolism means that character is not transferable (*Christ's Object Lessons*, p. 413). It is for these reasons that the apostle Paul admonishes us to examine ourselves, whether we be in the faith (2 Cor. 13:5).

The Midnight Cry is a message that points to the imminent close of probation. The parable states that, while the foolish virgins went to buy oil, the virgins who were ready went into the marriage with the Bridegroom, and the door was shut (Matt. 25:10). We need to make our preparations now for, when the great final test comes at the close of human probation, it will be too late (*Christ's Object Lessons*, p. 412).

And what is the great final test? God has revealed to us that the image of the beast [the Sunday law] is the great test that will decide the eternal destiny of God's people. Consider the following inspired statements: "The Lord has shown me clearly that the image of the beast will be formed before probation closes, for it is to be the great test for the people of God, by which their eternal destiny will be decided" (*Selected Messages*, book 2, p. 81). "We are to warn men and women against the worship of the beast and his image—against the worship of the idol Sunday" (*Christ Triumphant*, p. 178). "But in the very act of enforcing a religious duty by secular power, the churches would themselves form an image to the beast; hence the enforcement of Sunday-keeping in the United States would be an enforcement of the worship of the beast and his image" (*The Great Controversy*, p. 448). "The great issue so near at hand [enforcement of Sunday laws] will weed out those whom God has not appointed and He will have a pure, true, sanctified ministry prepared for the latter rain" (*Selected Messages*, book 3, p. 385). "The Sabbath will be the great test of loyalty, for it is the point of truth especially controverted. When the final test shall be brought to bear upon men, then the line of distinction will be drawn between those who serve God and those who serve Him not" (*The Great Controversy*, p. 605).

The Sunday law is the test that the people of God must pass before they are sealed (*Maranatha*, p. 164). When the enforcement of Sunday keeping goes into effect, the faithful of God will receive the seal of God in their foreheads. Ellen White wrote: "When the decree [the Sunday law] goes forth, and the stamp is impressed, their character will remain pure and spotless for eternity" (*Christian Experience and Teachings of Ellen White*, p. 191). The professed people of God, who do not have sufficient oil, are those without the necessary preparation to meet the test. It is evident that we cannot prepare to meet the Bridegroom when we awaken to hear the proclamation of the Midnight Cry. God has forewarned us that, in a crisis, character is only revealed; it cannot then be developed (*Christ's Object Lessons*, p. 412).

The proclamation of the Midnight Cry will commence when the enforcement of Sunday observance goes into effect. The Sunday law will be the great test for the professed people of God by which their eternal destiny will be decided, for it will reveal who has their loyalty. It is the event that signals the closing of probation for Seventh-day Adventists, and the close of probation for the professed people of God will come before the general close of probation. Ellen White called attention to the opportunity in God's great mercy when she wrote: "His heart of mercy is touched, His hand is still stretched out to save, while the door is closed to those who would not enter. Large numbers will be admitted who in these last days hear the truth for the first time" (Letter 103, 1903).

So then, how will the Midnight Cry be given, and what evidences will attend its proclamation? During the services of the earthly sanctuary, the children of Israel were connected with their high priest by the sounding of the bells hanging from his robe. As the high priest was interceding on their behalf, the people were able to discern his movements in the Holy and Most Holy Places. In hearing the sound, the children of Israel would be able to anticipate the closing of the work of the high priest and his coming out to the waiting congregation.

What do the bells represent for us today? What helps us to know the movements of our High Priest in the heavenly sanctuary? Are there literal bells from Christ's robe that sound forth from heaven above? No, but just as the priest's bells helped ancient Israel to stay connected to the mediation of the high priest in the earthly sanctuary, so now does prophecy help us to know that Jesus' ministration in the heavenly sanctuary is coming to a close and that He is soon to return to His waiting church on earth.

Revelation 14:7 declares: "Saying with a loud voice, Fear God, and give glory to him; for the hour of his judgment is come: and worship him that made heaven, and earth, and the sea, and the fountains of waters." This verse announces the commencement of the investigative judgment as Jesus moved from the Holy Place into the Most Holy Place. The prophecy of Daniel 8:14 declared when this was to take place: "And he said unto me, Unto two thousand and three hundred days; then shall the sanctuary be cleansed." The prophecy began in 457 BC with the going forth to restore and rebuild Jerusalem under the decree of King Artaxerxes, and it extended up to 1844. Jesus' work of cleansing the sanctuary and His intercession for us before the throne of God commenced in the autumn of that year. The prophet Daniel saw this cleansing in vision and declared it in Daniel 7:13, "I saw in the night visions, and, behold, one like the Son of man came with the clouds of heaven, and came to the Ancient of days, and they brought him near before him." Malachi 3:1 captures the same event: "… and the Lord, whom ye seek, shall suddenly come to his temple, even the messenger of the covenant, whom ye delight in: behold, he shall come, saith the LORD of hosts."

In review, we note that the bells hanging from the priestly garment connected ancient Israel to the intercessory work of the high priest in the earthly sanctuary. By the sounding of the bells, Israel was able to anticipate the closing of the ministration in the Most Holy Place and the return of the high priest to the waiting congregation. The bells worn by the high priest serve as a symbolic type of prophecy, which connects God's people to Jesus as He ministers on their behalf in the heavenly sanctuary. By a study of the prophetic word, we may be acquainted with His closing work in the Most Holy Place and know when His return to earth is near. The apostle Peter wrote: "We have also a more sure word of prophecy; whereunto ye do well that ye take heed, as unto a light that shineth in a dark place, until the day dawn, and the day star arise in your hearts" (2 Peter 1:19). The dawning of that day refers to the second coming of Christ in power and glory.

Enough has been revealed in prophecy that we may know when we have come to the last generation that will be alive at Christ's second coming. Seventh-day Adventist pioneer J. N. Loughborough declared: "In response to the question of the disciples, 'What shall be the sign of thy coming, and of the end of the world?' the Saviour gave them a list of the events that were to transpire down through the great tribulation that should come upon the church, and the definite signs that would occur. When these appeared, they might know that his coming was near, even at the doors, and that the generation that saw them would not pass off the stage of action until he came" (Loughborough, p. 68). We conclude that the Midnight Cry will be given in conjunction with the prophecies that validate the closing intercessory work of our High Priest in the heavenly sanctuary and His imminent return to earth.

Chapter 12.

Conclusions

Each of the ancient prophets wrote less for their own time than for those coming after them and especially for the generation that would live during the closing scenes of earth's history (*The Signs of the Times*, Jan. 13, 1898). They prophesied for our day, foretelling when "the great day of the Lord" would be at hand (Zeph. 1:14). The books of Joel, Luke, James, and Zephaniah have given us prophetic signs that we may know when His coming is near, even at the doors.

The global financial crisis of 2008 was a prophetic event indicating that Jesus arrived "at the door" and that this present generation will not pass until He returns in the clouds of heaven. Jesus declared, "So likewise ye, when ye shall see all these things, know that it is near, even at the doors. Verily I say unto you, This generation shall not pass, till all these things be fulfilled" (Matt. 24:33, 34). We are bidden to watch because we do not know when the master of the house cometh—at even or at midnight, at the cockcrowing or in the morning (Mark 13:35). The hours of a typical watch are divided into four periods: (1) the evening watch, 6:00 p.m. to 9:00 p.m.; (2) the midnight hour, 9:00 p.m. to 12:00 a.m.; (3) the cock-crowing, 12:00 a.m. to 3:00 a.m.; and (4) the morning watch, 3:00 a.m. to 6:00 a.m. Because of these divisions, I feel that we should divide the last generation (a biblical generation being forty years) as follows:

evening, 2008–2018; midnight, 2018–2028; the cockcrowing, 2028–2038; and the morning, 2038–2048. Although prophecy does not reveal the day or the hour of His coming, it does provide an approximation of time that we may know when we have come to the generation that will not pass before Christ returns in the clouds of glory.

The apostle Paul wrote that God "will finish the work and cut it short in righteousness, because a short work will the Lord make upon the earth" (Rom. 9:28). So "knowing the time, that now it is high time to awake out of sleep: for now is our salvation nearer than when we believed" (Rom. 13:11). God's sleeping children of Laodicea would do well to anoint their eyes with eyesalve that they may discern the signs of the times. To be as "the children of Issachar, which were men that had understanding of the times, to know what Israel ought to do" (1 Chron. 12:32).

Joel declared, "Blow the trumpet in Zion, and sound an alarm in my holy mountain: let all the inhabitants of the land tremble: for the day of the Lord cometh, for it is nigh at hand" (Joel 2:1). The watchmen on the walls of Zion need to sound an alarm throughout the length and breadth of the land, declaring to the people that "the great day of the Lord is near" (Zeph. 1:14). Having the light of the third angel's message, we are obligated to impart the truth to others. May we do our duty in warning the world of Christ's soon return.

We conclude with the words of Joel:

Therefore also now, saith the LORD, turn ye even to me with all your heart, and with fasting, and with weeping, and with mourning: And rend your heart, and not your garments, and turn unto the LORD your God: for he is gracious and merciful, slow to anger, and of great kindness, and repenteth him of the evil. Who knoweth if he will return and repent, and leave a blessing behind him; even a meat offering and a drink offering unto the LORD your God? Blow the trumpet in Zion, sanctify a fast, call a solemn assembly: Gather the people, sanctify the congregation, assemble the elders, gather the children, and those that suck the breasts: let the bridegroom go forth of his chamber, and the bride out of her closet. Let the priests, the ministers of the LORD, weep between the porch and the altar, and let them say, Spare thy people, O LORD, and give not thine heritage to reproach. (Joel 2:13–17)

Bibliography

Emmerson, W. L. *The Reformation and the Advent Movement*.
Hagerstown, MD: Review and Herald Publishing Association,
1983.

Fortin, Denis. "Ellen G. White and Seventh-day Adventist
Doctrines: Her role in the development of distinctive beliefs."
Adapted from Roger W. Coon's lecture outline, "Ellen G.
White and SDA Doctrine-Part I: God's FIRST Priority in the
First 20 Years," April 18, 1995. Available online at http://1ref.
us/bn, accessed 5/10/16.

Froom, Le Roy Edwin. *The Prophetic Faith of Our Fathers*, vol. 4.
Washington, DC: Review and Herald Publishing Association,
1954.

Greenhouse, Steven. "With Day of Protests, Fast-Food Workers
Seek More Pay." *The New York Times*, Nov. 29, 2012.
Available online at http://1ref.us/bo, accessed 4/24/16.

Kirkham, Chris and Samantha Masunaga. "Why the success of the $15 minimum wage movement has surprised its leaders." *Los Angeles Times*, Nov. 11, 2015. Available online at http://1ref.us/bp, accessed 4/24/16.

Liddell, Henry George, and Robert Scott. *A Greek-English Lexicon*. 8th Edition. New York: American Book Company, 1882.

Loughborough, J. N. *The Great Second Advent Movement Its Rise and Progress*. Ringgold, GA: TEACH Services Inc., 2013.

"Minimum Wage Protests Hit Cities across U.S." NBCNews.com, Dec. 4, 2014. Available online at http://1ref.us/bq, accessed 4/24/16.

Morgenson, Gretchen, and Joshua Rosner. *Reckless Endangerment: How Outsized Ambition, Greed, and Corruption Led to Economic Armageddon*. New York, NY: Times Books, 2011.

Nichol, Francis D., ed. *The Seventh-day Adventist Bible Commentary*, vol. 4. Washington, DC: Review and Herald Publishing Association, 1957.

———. *The Seventh-day Adventist Bible Commentary*, vol. 5. Washington, DC: Review and Herald Publishing Association, 1957.

———. *The Seventh-day Adventist Bible Commentary*, vol. 7. Washington, DC: Review and Herald Publishing Association, 1957.

Riley, Charles. *"IMF: The World Economy is worse off than we thought." CNN Money*, January 20, 2015. Available online at http://1ref.us/br, accessed 4/24/16.

"Scribe." Wikipedia. Available online at http://1ref.us/bs, accessed 4/24/16.

Smith, Uriah. *Daniel and the Revelation*. Battle Creek, MI: Review and Herald Publishing Association, 1897.

"Tell." Merriam-Webster Dictionary. Available online at http://1ref.us/bt, accessed 4/24/16.

"Watch Out: It is only a matter of time before the next recession strikes." *The Economist*, June 13, 2015.

White, Ellen G. "A Call to Service." *The Watchman*, June 18, 1907.

———. *Christian Experience and Teaching of Ellen G. White*. Mountain View, CA: Pacific Press Publishing Association, 1940.

———. "The Christian Pathway." *Signs of the Times*, March 6, 1884.

———. *Christ's Object Lessons*. Washington, DC: Review and Herald Publishing Association, 1941.

———. "Christ, the Teacher of Righteousness." *The Review and Herald*, August 6, 1895.

———. *Christ Triumphant*. Hagerstown, MD: Review and Herald Publishing Association, 1999.

———. *Counsels for the Church*. Nampa, ID: Pacific Press Publishing Association, 1991.

———. *Counsels on Health*. Nampa, ID: Pacific Press Publishing Association, 1957.

———. *Counsels to Writers and Editors*. Nashville, TN: Southern Publishing Association, 1946.

———. *Early Writings*. Washington, DC: Review and Herald Publishing Association, 1882.

———. *Evangelism*. Washington, DC: Review and Herald Publishing Association, 1946.

———. *The Great Controversy*. Mountain View, CA: Pacific Press Publishing Association, 1911.

———. "Heart Piety Essential." *The Signs of the Times*, April 2, 1896.

———. *Last Day Events*. Boise, ID: Pacific Press Publishing Association, 1992.

———. *Life Sketches of Ellen G. White*. Mountain View, CA: Pacific Press Publishing Association, 1915.

———. *Manuscript Releases*, vol. 1. Silver Spring, MD: Ellen G. White Estate, 1981.

———. *Manuscript Releases*, vol. 2. Silver Springs, MD: Ellen G. White Estate, 1987.

———. *Manuscript Releases*, vol. 9. Silver Spring, MD: Ellen G. White Estate, 1990.

———. *Manuscript Releases*, vol. 13. Silver Spring, MD: Ellen G. White Estate, 1987.

———. *Manuscript Releases*, vol. 16. Silver Spring, MD: Ellen G. White Estate, 1990.

———. *Manuscript Releases*, vol. 19. Silver Spring, MD: Ellen G. White Estate, 1990.

———. *Maranatha: The Lord Is Coming*. Washington, DC: Review and Herald Publishing Association, 1976.

———. "Nearness of the End." *The Review and Herald*, March 14, 1912.

———. *Prophets and Kings*. Mountain View, CA: Pacific Press Publishing Association, 1917.

———. *The Publishing Ministry*. Hagerstown, MD: Review and Herald Publishing Association, 1983.

———. "The Righteousness of Christ." *The Review and Herald*, Aug. 19, 1890.

———. *Selected Messages*, book 2. Washington, DC: Review and Herald Publishing Association, 1958.

———. *Selected Messages*, book 3. Washington, DC: Review and Herald Publishing Association, 1980.

———. "The Stone of Witness." *The Signs of the Times*, May 26, 1881.

———. *The Story of Jesus*. Nashville, TN: Southern Publishing Association, 1949.

———. "A Symbol of the Final Destruction." *The Signs of the Times*, Dec. 29, 1890.

———. *Testimonies for the Church*, vol. 1. Mountain View, CA: Pacific Press Publishing Association, 1881, 1902, 1948.

———. *Testimonies for the Church*, vol. 6. Mountain View, CA: Pacific Press Publishing Association, 1901.

———. *Testimonies for the Church*, vol. 9. Mountain View, CA: Pacific Press Publishing Association, 1909.

———. "The Way, the Truth, and the Life." *The Signs of the Times*, Jan. 13, 1898.

White, James, Ellen Gould White, and Joseph Bates. "A Word to the Little Flock." Ringgold, GA: TEACH Services Inc., 2014.

We invite you to view the complete
selection of titles we publish at:

www.ASPECTBooks.com

Scan with your mobile
device to go directly
to our website.

Please write or email us your praises, reactions,
or thoughts about this or any other book we publish at:

AB **ASPECT Books**
www.ASPECTBooks.com

info@ASPECTBooks.com

ASPECT Books titles may be purchased in bulk for
educational, business, fund-raising, or sales promotional use.
For information, please e-mail:

BulkSales@ASPECTBooks.com

Finally, if you are interested in seeing
your own book in print, please contact us at

publishing@ASPECTBooks.com

We would be happy to review your manuscript for free.

www.ingramcontent.com/pod-product-compliance
Lightning Source LLC
Chambersburg PA
CBHW060444090426
42733CB00011B/2376